Congratulations Graduate...

Congratulations, Graduate!

LET THE JOURNEY BEGIN

by Troy Johnson

BRISTOL PARK BOOKS

First Bristol Park Books edition
published in 2015

Bristol Park Books
252 W. 38th Street
NYC, NY 10018

Bristol Park Books is a registered trademark
of Bristol Park Books, Inc.

Library of Congress Control Number: 2014959399

ISBN: 978-0-88486-584-1
E-Book ISBN: 978-0-88486-585-8

Text and cover designed by Cindy LaBreacht

Printed in the United States of America

To_____

From_____

Date_____

Contents

Foreword

Go ahead and celebrate! You deserve it. You've reached, for most, that first key milestone along the journey. Officially, you now begin a more independent path. There are questions like: Are you ready? Are you nervous? What lies ahead? What are you leaving behind? Have you thought much about it or are you just taking life in stride? These questions now become more relevant and important.

There's no absolute right or wrong answer. It all depends on...yes, I know, you've heard it a lot lately..."what are you going to do now?" and "where are you going?" Don't worry. It's the common questions that everyone is asking and being asked.

Here's the good news. You don't have to have it all figured out. Walking into life's journey will help define your next steps. However, making the right decisions will also be important. It will allow you to develop a life plan and pursue it with passion. These are key components in helping you achieve your goals and objectives.

Think of it this way: How did you feel after putting a lot of effort into a huge test or a key term paper or even after the last game of the season? Most likely, it was a sigh of relief and depending on the result your reaction was a direct response to the outcome. More importantly, there was a time to respond with celebration or if the end result didn't meet your satisfaction... as the saying goes, "better luck next time"

This is similar to life, and it primarily depends on how you set your expectations as well as how you deliver the results. But in reality, how we perform in life is measured "in the between"— what we do that leads up to the outcome.

But for now, it's a time to celebrate your accomplishments. Take a sigh of relief and enjoy the moment. You have a lot of life in front of you!

Congratulations, Graduate!

TROY JOHNSON

Let the Celebration Begin

THERE ARE SPECIFIC MOMENTS in life that are worth celebrating: holidays, birthdays, significant events, achieving accomplishments, receiving awards, and many more. Each is a memorable episode that is worth celebrating. And for how long it seems for an event to arrive, it's gone even quicker with only well-wishes and memories to cherish.

So don't just let the celebration begin. Allow it to be a defining moment, representing the significance of a job well done. Graduation is meant to be a time of recognition. It is meant to be an outward expression of honoring your efforts and accomplishments.

This is one of life's shining moments—made for celebrating. Go ahead, let it out and enjoy the time with friends, family, and classmates. Don't get caught up with "what's next in life." Instead, slow down and embrace the occasion.

This is what graduation celebrations are meant to accomplish. It's a collective effort that reflects the individual accomplishment. It is life's way of revealing that one segment of your journey has been conquered with several more ahead.

Stepping Up! Opportunities Around You

LISTEN CAREFULLY to successful people all over the world and they will tell you one thing: "Opportunity quietly surrounds you." Information and knowledge are within your reach. Prosperity is silently knocking at your door. Victory mysteriously awaits you. Subtle and vague as it may seem, there is no scarcity of success. It is available to you. The only real problem is how we choose to respond to the unlimited abundance that is ours for the taking.

> Do we accept it or reject it?
> Do we allow it or resist it?
> Do we demand it or dismiss it?
> Do we take it in or turn it away?

We live in a society where people are always chasing the next opportunity to get ahead. Proactive people are advancing themselves without being asked or encouraged. They just do it, often surprising the people around them. This illustrates that we do not need permission to step up. We do not need to be told to do it, or even asked. We can apply ourselves in ways that we may not have even imagined. The key is to know that we can step up and then know how!

THE MAN WHO grasps an opportunity as it is paraded before him, nine times out of ten makes a success; but the man who makes his own opportunities is a sure-fire success.

DALE CARNEGIE

New Beginnings

Just because this is a book addressing "the graduate" and will feature a variety of topics, it's likely that a brand new phase of life is just around the corner. If so, congratulations! It also means that you've graduated *from* something (or somewhere) to something else (or someplace else). You're about to embark on your next big adventure.

As you think about your future—and as you consider the countless opportunities that will be woven into the fabric of the days ahead—be sure to remember what brought you to where you are currently at. When you do, try to focus on the things that will best lead you down the right path.

Perhaps your desire is to change the direction of your life. Or perhaps you're determined to make major modifications in the way you live.

Or what about the way you think? If so, you can do it! However don't expect change to be easy or instant. Life doesn't necessarily measure on the "easy scale." Instead work in conjunction with life's demands, expectations, and even the rules that apply most to you.

TIMELESS WISDOM

As you graduate into a new phase of life, let focus and a balanced life be your key contributors. Most importantly, know who you are and stay true to who you are. These are the things that really matter.

BEGIN SOMEWHERE: you cannot build a reputation on what you intend to do.

JAMES RUSSELL LOWELL

SO WHAT DO WE DO? Anything. Something. So long as we just don't sit there. If we screw up, start over. Try something else. If we wait until we've satisfied all the uncertainties, it may be too late.

LEE IACOCCA

DO WHAT YOU CAN, with what you have, where you are.

THEODORE ROOSEVELT

LIFE BEGINS when you do.

HUGH DOWNS

Opportunity Knocks

Opportunities and motivation are connected. Motivated people see opportunities, and opportunities are often what motivate people.

> Great attitudes precede great opportunities.
>
> Who you are determines what you see.
>
> Today is the best day for an opportunity.
>
> Opportunity always takes "now" for an answer.
>
> Opportunities are the result of pluck, not luck.

The people who succeed seek out opportunities, and if they can't find them, they create them. Opportunities don't present themselves in ideal circumstances. If you wait for all the lights to turn green, you will never leave where you are.

Opportunities without commitment will be your loss. Abandoned opportunities are never lost—they are simply pursued by the competition.

Opportunity is birthed out of problems. If you're looking for a BIG opportunity, find a BIG problem. Opportunities either multiply or disappear. The more opportunities you pursue, the more you find behind them.

Opportunities must be nourished if they are to be sustainable. Peter Drucker, the father of modern management would say, "Feed an opportunity; starve a problem."

TIMELESS WISDOM

The world is full of abundance and opportunity, but far too many people come to the fountain of life with a glass instead of a pitcher... a teaspoon instead of a steam shovel. They expect little and as a result they get little in return.

OPPORTUNITIES are swarming around us all the time, thicker than gnats at sundown. We walk through a cloud of them.

HENRY VAN DYKE

TOO OFTEN the opportunity knocks, but by the time you disengage the chain, push back the bolt, unhook the two locks and shut off the burglar alarms, it's too late.

RITA COOLIDGE

OPPORTUNITIES should never be lost because they can hardly be regained.

WILLIAM PENN

PEOPLE WHO HAVE GIVEN UP are ruled by their darkest mistakes, worst failures and deepest regrets. If you want to be successful, then be driven by your finest thoughts, your highest enthusiasm, your greatest optimism, and your most triumphant experiences.

JIM THORPE

Two Steps Forward

Do more than exist: *live*
Do more than touch: *feel*
Do more than look: *observe*
Do more than read: *absorb*
Do more than listen: *reflect*
Do more than listen: *understand*
Do more than think: *reflect*
Do more than just talk: *say something*

TIMELESS WISDOM

Whatever you do, do it with all your
might. Work at it, early and late.
In season and out of season, not leaving
a stone unturned, and never deferring
for a single hour that which can be done
just as well as now.

WHY WAIT? Quit practicing what you are
going to do and just do it.

MARILYN GREY

SOMEWHERE in your make-up there lies sleeping the seed of achievement which, if aroused and put into action, would carry you to heights such as you may never have to attain.

NAPOLEON HILL

THE WAY to get started is to quit talking and begin doing.

WALT DISNEY

YOU DON'T have to be great to get started, but you have to get started to be great.

LES BROWN

Energized for Life

Is your life in acceleration mode or on auto pilot or worse, in idle mode? If you're gauges are pointing towards the empty mark, then it's time to get fueled up and find the things that are going to serve as motivators to energize your life.

Whether you are drawing your energy from external motivation or through inner strength, or both, don't stop whatever source that is fueling you with increased momentum.

The key is to seek out what works best and stick with it! You would rather go through your week with a greater level of energy to keep you focused, upbeat, and productive.

TIMELESS WISDOM

Feeling exhausted! Try this: Get more sleep each night. Begin a program of regular, sensible exercise. Avoid harmful food and drink. And find a way to make stress a choice. Try it for 30 days and you'll begin to see and more importantly feel the results. Seems simple? Yes. That's the point!

ENTHUSIASM finds the opportunities, and energy makes the most of them.

HENRY S. HASKINS

DO A LITTLE MORE than average and from that point on our progress multiplies itself out of all proportion to the effort put in.

PAUL J. MEYER

START by doing what's necessary;
then do what's possible; and suddenly
you are doing the impossible.

SAINT FRANCIS OF ASSISI

LIFE IS what we make it: always has been, always will be.

ANNA MARY ROBERTSON (AKA: GRANDMA MOSES)

Anticipating Great Things Ahead

You have been given talents and opportunities that are uniquely yours. Are you willing to use your gifts in ways that benefit you and your future? And are you willing to commit to the discipline required to develop your talents and craft your skills?

As you seek to expand your talents, you will undoubtedly encounter stumbling blocks along the way, such as the fear of rejection or the fear of failure. When you do, don't stumble. Rather continue to refine your skills and use them to extend opportunities that benefit you, the people around you, and the causes you choose to participate in.

And when the time is right, you will be in a position to be recognized and to be used in ways that bring opportunities.

Let the journey prepare you for what is next because there will be times that afford you the chance to grow and refine your strengths, skills, and talents.

TIMELESS WISDOM

You're the sole owner of your own talents and opportunities. You have been given your own particular gifts—the rest is up to you. Along the way, you'll have a chance to make a difference and impact lives—including yours.

WHAT LIES BEHIND US and what lies before us are tiny matters compared to what lies within us.

RALPH WALDO EMERSON

DON'T BE AFRAID to take a big step if needed. You can't cross a chasm in two small steps.

ANONYMOUS

ACTIONS are seeds of fate. Seeds grow into destiny.

HARRY S. TRUMAN

THE ONLY QUESTION in life is whether or not you are going to answer a hearty "Yes!" to your adventure.

JOSEPH CAMPBELL

Priorities
First

TO REMAIN FOCUSED and on track, making a list of priorities is a must. Then learn to put things first. If you reverse the process and try to put things in order without first prioritizing, your focus turns to "what needs to be done" versus "how to get it done" most efficiently and with effective results.

In life we tend to gravitate towards "doing" and forget our priorities. Does the following list read familiar?

> Easy things first
> Fun things first
> Urgent things first
> Hard things first
> First things first

The above actions can serve as priorities, but often times we substitute our own list, in our own way, and by our own definition, which often times is far from any sort of priority order.

Whether you are developing a set of priorities for your life or realigning them to better suit your life, its value, and desired results, you must first learn priority order. Quickly you will begin to experience the difference between mere activity and accomplishment.

We tend to spend too much time sifting through the many things that demand and occupy our time. It's important to understand not only what needs to be done but possibly more importantly what doesn't need to be done at all.

This starts with a passion to excel. When you focus your passion on what's most important, your priorities will quickly take shape and become the priority.

Focus on Priorities

What is your focus today? Are you willing to focus your thoughts and energies on the most important tasks? Or will you turn your thoughts to other things?

Today is a chance to recognize that priorities make a difference versus just a set of tasks or happenings that potentially create a "time suck" that prove to keep you busy versus productive—the things that truly count.

Go ahead and focus your thoughts and actions on the things that are going to propel you forward. In a life transition, it's key to recognize your priorities but even more important to focus and accomplish tasks that turn into opportunities, achievement, and yes, that build a road of success in your journey.

It has been often said, "Whatever we focus on determines what we become." What will you end up becoming? Focus on the things that will ultimately determine your outcome.

TIMELESS WISDOM

First focus on priorities and then everything else will become what you need to do.

NO MATTER how much time you've wasted in the past, you still have all of tomorrow. Success depends upon using it wisely by planning and setting priorities.

DENIS WAITLEY

THE WAY YOU SEE your future determines your thinking today. Your thinking today determines your performance today. Your performance in the todays of your life determines your future.

ZIG ZIGLAR

YOU ARE the way you are because that's the way you want to be. If you really wanted to be any different, you would be in the process of changing right now.

FRED SMITH

First Things First

Have you taken time to sit down and write out a list of priorities that can help guide and prioritize your life? If you have, then you know the importance of the exercise in helping you walk on a clearer path of goals and objectives in your life.

So often, we want to jump ahead without doing the planning and preparation that allows us to live out and achieve our priorities. In doing so, it doesn't work out so well.

If you enjoy running, you know that it takes time to build up stamina, leg strength, and other muscle memory that help you achieve a certain distance. If you just go out and run one or two miles (or more) you may be able to finish, but what are you putting at risk? Without the proper training—in building up to a certain distance—our bodies are not as conditioned as if we took the appropriate measures leading up to days and/or weeks of preparation.

It's the same in life. Take a step by step, first things first, approach. It's a lot easier to achieve our goals and objectives when we plan and prepare versus not prioritizing and just thinking we can do it.

TIMELESS WISDOM

Sometimes, life doesn't require or expect a priority order. However, with priorities in place, we are that much more ready to tackle and achieve our goals with greater confidence and ability.

THE MOST IMPORTANT thing about goals is having one. The most important thing about achieving your goals is through priorities.

GEOFFREY F. ABERT

RUN YOUR DAY by the clock and your life with priorities.

ZIG ZIGLAR

WHEN YOU BELIEVE and think "I can" you activate your motivation, commitment, confidence, concentration and enthusiasm—all of which relate directly to achievement.

DR. JERRY LYNCH

Decisions 101

From the instant you wake in the morning until the close of day, you have the opportunity to make countless decisions. Decisions about the things you do. Decisions about the words you speak. And decisions about the thoughts you choose to think.

If you're facing a major life decision, here are some practical things you can do:

Gather as much information as you can

Don't be too impulsive

Rely on the advice of trusted friends and mentors

Continue to seek guidance

Trust the quiet inner voice of your conscience, and

When the time for action arrives, act. Procrastination is the enemy of progress; don't let it defeat you.

People who can never quite seem to make up their minds usually make themselves miserable. So when in doubt, be decisive. It's the decent and best way to live.

TIMELESS WISDOM

Slow down! If you're about to make an important decision, don't be impulsive. Remember, big decisions have big consequences, and if you don't think about the consequences now, you may pay a big price later.

WE ARE FREE up to the point of choice; then the choice controls the chooser.

MARY CROWLEY

WHEN YOU HAVE a choice and don't make it, that is, in itself, a choice

WILLIAM JAMES

CHOICE, not chance determines human destiny

ROBERT W. ELLIS

BE WILLING to make decisions. That's the most important quality of a good leader. Don't fall victim to what I call the ready-aim-aim-aim syndrome. You must be willing to fire.

T. BOONE PICKENS

Find Your Vision

One of the great dreamers of the twentieth century was Walt Disney. Any person who could create the first sound cartoon, first all-color cartoon, and first animated feature-length motion picture is definitely someone with vision. But Disney's greatest masterpieces of vision were Disneyland and Walt Disney World. And the spark for that vision came from an unexpected place.

Back when Walt's two daughters were young, he used to take them to an amusement park in the Los Angeles area on Saturday mornings. His girls loved it, and he did as well. Amusement parks are a kid's paradise, with wonderful atmosphere: the smell of popcorn and cotton candy, the gaudy colors of signs advertising rides, and the sound of kids screaming as the roller coaster plummets over a hill.

Walt was especially captivated by the carousel. As he approached it, he saw a blur of bright images racing around to the tune of energetic music. But when he got closer and the carousel stopped, he could see that his eye had been fooled. He observed shabby horses with cracked and chipped paint. And he noticed that only the horses on the outside row moved up and down. The others stood lifeless, bolted to the floor.

The cartoonist's disappointment inspired him with a grand vision. In his mind's eye he could see an amusement park where the illusion didn't evaporate, where children and adults could enjoy a carnival atmosphere without the seedy side that accompanied some circuses or traveling carnivals. Walt's dream became Disneyland.

For Disney, vision was never a problem. Because of his creativity and desire for excellence, he always saw what could be.

TIMELESS WISDOM

If you lack vision, look inside yourself.
Draw on your natural gifts and desires.
Look to your calling if you have one.
And if you still don't sense a vision of
your own, then consider hooking up with
a person whose vision resonates with
you. Remember, vision without execution
is just seeing and not believing. Don't let
your dreams fall to the side because you
don't pursue them.

A VISION is a clearly-articulated, results-oriented
picture of a future you intend to create.
It is a dream with direction.

JESSE STONER ZEMEL

A VISION without a task is but a dream.
A task without a vision is drudgery.
A vision and a task are the hope of the world.

QUOTE ON A CHURCH WALL IN SUSSEX, ENGLAND

Using Your Talents

We all possess special talents. Some people describe "talents" as "our gifts that we were born with." No matter what we label them, talents or gifts, they are the internal components that help drive personal success. However, life doesn't guarantee that you'll achieve success. You have to identify, nurture, and use your talents consistently to better recognize how to best maximize the use of them.

Today, make a promise that you will earnestly seek to discover your God-given talents. Then nourish those talents and increase them to your full potential. In order to achieve peak performance, over time, you'll have to discover your own abilities and practices. Yes, it's part of the process of learning and using your talents. And once you hit that "sweet spot," you'll quickly realize how much of a "life benefit" they become.

Don't forget to nourish and grow your talents. It may be the best use of your energy and resources to achieve personal success.

TIMELESS WISDOM

Remember that you have a unique array of talents and opportunities. If you use your gifts wisely, they multiply. If you misuse them or ignore them, they can be lost.

A GIFTED LEADER is one who is capable of touching your heart.

JACOB SAMUEL POTOFSKY

DO WHAT YOU DO so well that they want to see it again and bring their friends.

WALT DISNEY

EACH OF US are given certain attributes, characteristics and talents. It's ours to use them but if you don't, you'll never know your full potential.

CHARLIE "TREMENDOUS" JONES

The Pitfalls of Procrastination

The habit of procrastination takes a two-fold toll on its victims. First, important work goes unfinished, and more importantly, valuable energy is wasted in the process of putting off the things that remain undone.

Procrastination results from an individual's short-sighted attempt to postpone temporary discomfort. What results is a senseless cycle of:

> Delay, followed by
>
> Worry, followed by
>
> Panic combined with often futile attempts to "catch up."

Procrastination is, at its core, a struggle against oneself. The only antidote is to step up and create action.

Once you acquire the habit of doing what needs to be done and when it needs be done, you will avoid untold trouble, worry, and stress. So learn to defeat procrastination by paying less attention to your fears and more attention to your responsibilities. Life doesn't procrastinate—neither should you.

It's easy to put off unpleasant tasks until "later." A far better strategy is first, do the unpleasant work and then enjoy the rest of your day. You may have heard of this saying, "Slay the dragons before noon or risk the dragons slaying you."

WHY WAIT? Life is not a dress rehearsal.

MARILYN GREY

PROCRASTINATION is opportunity's natural assassin.

VICTOR KIAM

GET ACTION. Do things: be sane,
don't waste away your time;
create, act, take a place wherever
you are and be somebody;
get action.

THEODORE ROOSEVELT

TAKE TIME to deliberate but when the time for action arrives, stop thinking and go in.

ANDREW JACKSON

Quality of Life... Simplicity

You live in a world where simplicity is in short supply. Think for a moment about the complexity of your everyday life and compare it to the lives of past generations. Certainly, you are the beneficiary of many technological innovations, but those have a price; in all likelihood, your world is highly complex.

Unless you take firm control of your time and your life, you may be overwhelmed by an ever-increasing tidal wave of complexity that threatens your happiness. So do yourself a favor; keep your life as simple as possible. Simplicity is, indeed, genius. By simplifying your life, you are destined to improve it.

The most powerful life is a simple life. The most powerful life is the life that knows where it's going; that knows where the source of strength is; it is the life that stays free of clutter and hurriedness.

Simplicity and peace are two concepts that are closely related. Complexity and peace are not.

UNTIL YOU make peace with who you are you will never be content with what you have.

DORIS MORTMAN

IT'S NOT what you know or who you know. It's what you are that finally counts.

ZIG ZIGLAR

SEEK TO DO GOOD and you will find that happiness will run after you.

JAMES FRANCIS CLARKE

REMEMBER, happiness doesn't depend on who you are or what you have, it depends solely upon what you think.

DALE CARNEGIE

Expecting the Best

What do you expect from the day ahead? Are you expecting to do wonderful things or are you living beneath a cloud of apprehension and doubt?

For optimists, they are always looking at the glass half full—the day full of opportunity, confidence walking into a meeting, believing you can achieve a daunting task, etc.

As we face the inevitable challenges of life, we must believe and reassure ourselves with the promises of the day so we can side step the pitfalls. When we do, we can expect the best, not only for the day ahead, but also for a lifetime.

TIMELESS WISDOM

Today, think about your role—your part in the story—and where you are in life. Now think about ways that you can worry less and begin to trust more in areas of your life.

INPUT INFLUENCES outlook, outlook influences output, and output determines outcome.

ANONYMOUS

FAITH BELIEVES in spite of circumstances and acts in spite of consequences.

ADRIAN ROGERS

GREAT STRENGTH comes from within not from without.

MARK BOWSER

HOW WE spend our days is, of course, how we spend our lives.

ANNIE DILLARD

The Details in
Being Diligent

WHEN STARTING a new initiative—job, college, project—the theory is to begin with a spirit of tenacity, energy, and diligence with the goal of getting started on the right foot. At least that is the goal. To get ahead, you have to do more than what is required, even expected.

It seems fairly simple right, yet I've noticed that most people do not follow or believe this simple philosophy. In fact, I noticed that most people have the exact opposite philosophy. It's easier to take the attitude of "if they paid me more..." or "if they told me more needed to be done.... then I would do more." These tend to be the same people who complain about all the things that go wrong.

Dr. Wayne Dyer said, "It is never crowded along the extra mile." Are you someone who continuously goes the extra mile?

Most successful people do more. They are the ones that arrive early and stay late if necessary. They think and act like winners, and they earn the rewards. They are not at this point because they're smarter or more gifted. They work harder. In the end, they earned it!

What can you expect if you adopt this philosophy and attitude of diligence? When you give more than expected, you are more likely to receive recognition and praise for a job well done.

Chances are you will never need to worry about things like your place on the team, your grades, or job security. You will be well respected by both your peers and those in leadership roles.

The philosophy is easy to understand. The key is accepting full responsibility for yourself and for the choices you make.

Be Diligent

The demands of life remind us again and again that the more we can live a focused and disciplined life, the further we can hit our stride in life's pursuits. Typically, we are not rewarded for acts of laziness, misbehavior, or apathy. To the contrary, we are expected to perform with dignity, integrity, and disciplined actions.

We live in a world in which leisure is glorified and indifference is often glamorized. But life's busyness and continued demands offer a different route to the often times commercialized picture of "easy street."

Life's greatest rewards seldom fall into our laps. To the contrary, our greatest accomplishments usually require a lot of work. After all, if we're being diligent about pursuing life with intention, our big plans will turn into even greater results.

TIMELESS WISDOM

When you take a disciplined approach to your life and your responsibilities, your rewards will be greater than you expected.

AND THEN SOME... these three little words are the secret to success. They are the difference between average "just doing" and "getting it done." The top people always do what is expected... and then some. They are thoughtful of others, and they are considerate and kind... and then some. They meet their responsibilities fairly and square... and then some. They are good friends and helpful neighbors... and then some. They can be counted on in an emergency... and then some. I am thankful for people like this, for they make the world a better place. Their spirit of diligence is summed up in these three words... and then some.

CARL HOLMES

WHATEVER the struggle, continue the climb. It may be only one step to the summit.

DIANE WESTLAKE

WE CAN DO anything we want to if we stick to it long enough

HELEN KELLER

Purpose Equals Growth

Each new day offers countless opportunities to seek out new ways to grow both personally and professionally. The same is true of the opposite. There are also countless opportunities to allow life to offer distractions that stray you far off the path leaving your goals and expectations behind only to see them in the rearview mirror.

At times, it seems as though we wander aimlessly in a wilderness of our own making versus a wide open market that offers various opportunities and the ability to fuel our confidence and our abilities for growth.

Consider the new growth that come with newly beginning experiences from opportunities that catapult us to new heights. This is where "finding your purpose" becomes such an important part of the equation. Often times, new opportunities come when we are willing to pause, focus, and hit the "restart button" again. It can be that easy. Seize the opportunity while you can. Tomorrow may indeed be too late.

TIMELESS WISDOM

No matter how badly you may fail (and it will happen), just get back up and begin again. A second chance opportunity is waiting to see how you respond and more importantly what you learn as an opportunity for seasoned growth.

IT IS NOT ENOUGH to being; continuance is necessary.... Success depends upon staying power. The reason for failure in most cases is lack of perseverance.

J.R. MILLER

SINGLENESS of purpose is one of the chief essentials for success in life, no matter what may be one's aim.

JOHN D. ROCKEFELLER

IT'S IN the struggle itself that you define yourself.

PAT BUCHANAN

THE ONLY difference between successful people and unsuccessful people is extraordinary determination.

MARY KAY ASH

Everyday Courage

We often think of courage as a quality required only in times of danger or stress. But courage is an everyday virtue, needed to live a life without regrets. Why do we need courage?

> We need courage to seek the truth when we know it may be painful.

> We need courage to change when it's easier to remain comfortable.

> We need courage to express our conviction when others challenge us.

> We need courage to overcome obstacles when progress will come no other way.

> We need courage to take the high road when others mistreat us or take advantage of us.

> We need courage to learn and grow when it will display our weakness.

> We need courage to lead when being in front makes us most vulnerable.

TIMELESS WISDOM

Courage is a special kind of knowledge; the knowledge of how to fear what ought to be feared, and how not to fear what ought not to be feared. From the knowledge comes an inner strength that subconsciously inspires us to push on in the face of great difficulty. What can seem impossible is often possible, with courage. —DAVID BEN-GURION

SUCCESS MEANS having the courage, the determination, and the will to become the person you believe you were meant to be.

GEORGE SHEEHAN

IF YOU COULD get up the courage to begin, then you have the courage to succeed.

DAVID VISCOTT

COURAGE is resistance to fear, master of fear— not absence of fear.

MARK TWAIN

COURAGE is the decision to place your dreams above your fears.

ANONYMOUS

Develop Best Practices

It's an old saying and a true one: "First, you make your habits, and then your habits make you." Some habits inevitably turn either into bad or best practices. It's up to you.

Easier said than done, right? If you sincerely desire to improve the way in which you manage your life, you must honestly examine the habits that you form and abandon the habits that cause you to stumble. If you trust your instincts and develop consistent actions, then over time, life habits become best practices.

Time will be the main measurement of which direction you take. Use time also as a means to develop best practices. If it takes 21 days to form a habit, then use this time frame to establish specific patterns that maximize the efficiencies of effectiveness towards abandoning any bad habits and forming those best practices.

Think of it this way: you will never change your life until you change what you do daily. To finish strong you have to first start.

TIMELESS WISDOM

Choose your habits carefully. Habits are easier to make than they are to break!

THE BEGINNING of a habit is like an invisible thread, but every time we repeat the act we strengthen the strand, add to it another filament, until it becomes a great cable that binds us irrevocably through thought and act.

ORRISON SWETT MARDEN

HABIT is stronger than reason.

GEORGE SANTAYANA

REPETITION is the mother of learning, the father of action, which makes it the architect of accomplishment.

ZIG ZIGLAR

IT IS JUST AS EASY to form a good habit as it is a bad one. And it is just as hard to break a good habit as a bad one. So get the good ones and keep them.

WILLIAM MCKINLEY

Ask for Directions

Before Google Maps, Siri, and GPS capabilities, there were printed maps or simply stopping and asking for directions. What happens when we choose to ignore the directions or simply not ask? We tend to get lost, get frustrated, and ultimately lose time, not arrive on time, or worse, miss something important—the start of a movie, an important meeting, or some other significant event.

Life is similar. If we don't plan out our route, follow a schedule, or ask for directions (or don't follow directions), we fail to find our destination. The 1980's movie, "Trains, Planes, and Automobiles" is a classic example of how we make life harder than it needs to be, or was it a movie depicting "sometimes you can't control what life throws at you." I believe it's both.

Even when we are intentional about seeking out the right directions to take, it doesn't always prove to be the best route. Circumstances do and will continue to get in the way of even perfect planning, directions, and intentions. All you can do is strive for the best situation, follow it, and trust that the outcome will lead to desired results.

TIMELESS WISDOM

Even though we may stop and ask for directions, we may still struggle to know exactly where to go because we don't follow the instructions. Stay on the guided path. Eventually, you'll arrive!

NOTHING SHAPES our journey through life so much as the questions we ask.

GREGG LEVOY

THE ART AND SCIENCE of asking questions is the source of all knowledge.

THOMAS BERGER

TO BE on a quest is nothing more or less than to become a seeker of information.

SAM KEEN

'HOW DO you know so much about everything?" was asked of a very wise and intelligent man; and the answer was "By never being afraid or ashamed to ask questions as to anything of which I was ignorant."

JOHN ABBOTT

Achieving Your Dreams

As you move forward in the pursuit of your dreams, you need to ask yourself, "Am I depending on factors within my control to achieve my dreams?"

People who build their dreams on reality take a very different approach to dreams than people who base them on fantasy. People who are successful in the long run don't leave everything to chance. They focus on what they can do; then they do it.

To achieve your dream, you not only need to work hard for it, but you also have to make sure it plays to your strengths. That means knowing what you can and cannot do. The first step in facing reality requires you to look at yourself realistically, to see yourself as you truly are.

The nature of self-evaluation has a profound effect on a person's values, beliefs, thinking, processes, feelings, needs, and goals. Focus on doing the things you love to do and build on your strengths.

TIMELESS WISDOM

When you build on your strengths, the activities using those strengths come more easily to you. To achieve your dream(s), you have to build on your strengths.

TO ACHIEVE anything significant, everyone needs a little imagination and a big dream.

NORMAN VINCENT PEALE

WHEN WE DARE to dream, many marvels can be accomplished. The trouble is, most people never start dreaming their impossible dream.

GLENN VAN EKEREN

BLESSED ARE THOSE who dream dreams and are willing to pay the price to make them come true.

HENRY VISCARDI JR.

THERE ARE NO limits to growth and human progress when men and women are free to follow their dreams.

RONALD REAGAN

Solving Problems

Life is an exercise in problem-solving. The question is not whether we will encounter problems. Rather, the real question is how we will address them.

When it comes to solving the problems of everyday living, we often know precisely what needs to be done, but we may be slow in doing it—especially if what needs to be done is difficult or uncomfortable for us. So we put off what should be done today for another day.

Doing "the right thing" usually means doing the uncomfortable work of confronting our problems sooner rather than later. So, what are you waiting on? Let the problem solving begin... now.

TIMELESS WISDOM

Everyone has problems, but not everyone deals with their problems in the same way. How you address your problems—whether you choose to avoid them or address them—determines how successfully—and how quickly—you overcome them.

IF YOU'RE TRYING to achieve, there will be roadblocks. I've had them; everybody has had them. But obstacles don't have to stop you. If you run into a wall, don't turn around and give up. Figure out how to climb it, go through it, or work around it.

MICHAEL JORDAN

OBSTACLES cannot crush me. Every obstacle yields to stern resolve. He who is fixed to a star does not change his mind.

LEONARDO DA VINCI

WE FIND no real satisfaction or happiness in life without obstacles to conquer and goals to achieve

MAXWELL MALTZ

The Power of Perseverance

A well-lived life calls for preparation, determination, and, of course, lots of perseverance. As a graduate, what brought you to this point? If it weren't for your tenacity to get through the hard times and persevere through the most difficult stages, you wouldn't be at this point in your life.

But as you've probably heard, your opportunity to exercise your power of perseverance is just beginning. As you face tough situations, remember, "No problem is too hard to handle." Often the best and only strategy is to walk through each step with an attitude of perseverance.

Without it, it's like having the wrong pair of football shoes on a wet and muddy field instead of cleats that dig in to the soil and provide traction. Perseverance is the traction you need to break through and handle the life challenges thrown your way.

TIMELESS WISDOM

Life is an exercise in perseverance. If you persevere, you win!

THE DIFFERENCE between the impossible and the possible lies in a person's determination.

TOMMY LASORDA

PERSEVERANCE is not a long race; it is many short races one after another.

WALTER ELLIOTT

PERSEVERANCE is a great element of success. IF you only knock long enough and loud enough at the gate, you are sure to wake somebody.

HENRY WADSWORTH LONGFELLOW

YOU JUST CAN'T BEAT the person who never gives up.

BABE RUTH

A Passion for Life

Are you enthusiastic about your life and for others? Hopefully you are. But if your zest for life has begun to erode or has already left, it is time to redirect your efforts and recharge your batteries. This means refocusing on blessings rather than on your problems.

How you approach your life is as important as how you live your life. Both invite a level of emotional engagement. What kind and how much is up to you. More importantly, are you pursuing life with intention? If so, is it with passion and purpose?

Life should never be an afterthought. Rather it needs to be your ultimate passion. When you become passionate about life and how you fit into its purpose, you'll find greater purpose in life too.

TIMELESS WISDOM

Don't wait for enthusiasm to find you... go looking for it. Look at your life and your relationships as exciting adventures. Don't wait for life to pursue you. Life is a journey. Make sure it includes the pursuit of a passionate purpose.

ENTHUSIASM is the inspiration of everything great. Without it no man is to be feared, and with it none despised.

CHRISTIAN N. BOVEE

NOTHING is so contagious as enthusiasm

EDWARD BULWER-LYTTON

FOLLOW your enthusiasm. It's something I've always believed in. Find those parts of your life you enjoy the most. Do what you enjoy doing.

JIM HENSON

A MAN will succeed at anything about which he is really enthusiastic.

CHARLES M. SCHWAB

Encouragement
Changes
Everything

EVERYONE NEEDS encouragement. And everyone—young or old, the successful or less-than-successful, unknown or famous—who receives encouragement is changed by it.

Encouragement's impact can be profound. A word of encouragement from a teacher to a child can change his life. Encouragement from a spouse can save a marriage...from a leader can inspire another to reach their potential...from a friend can reinforce the significance of the other.

The late Zig Ziglar said, "You never know when a moment and a few sincere words can have an impact on a life."

What does true encouragement look like—the kind that changes lives forever? To encourage people is to help them gain courage they might not otherwise possess—courage to face the day to day, to do what's right, to make risks, to make a difference. When we help people feel valuable, capable, and motivated we sometimes see their lives change forever, and we then see them go on to change the world.

No matter your role in life, you have the ability to encourage others to make a difference. Encouragement has the power to create an environment where people can become their best.

Finding Encouragement

Encouragement can change everything for the better. Encouragement also offers hope. Hope, like other human emotions, is contagious. If we associate with and around hope-filled, enthusiastic people, they will have a tendency to lift our spirits. But if we find ourselves spending too much time in the company of naysayers, pessimists, or cynics, our thoughts will tend to also become negative.

Ask yourself the question, "Are you a hopeful, optimistic person?" And do you associate with like-minded people? If so, then you're both wise and blessed.

We are constantly surrounded by negativity in our lives. We have to face the media, the undertone at work, continued problems within our circle of friends and family, as well as our own "stuff." Are you going to rise above and find the hope to encourage and inspire you? Try not to live in the alternative, which can lead to misery and discouragement.

When things go wrong, it's easy to become discouraged. But those who discover a path of hope will find a greater road of encouragement.

A SMILE of encouragement at the right moment may act like sunlight on a closed up flower; it may be the turning point for a struggling life

ALFRED A. MONTAPERT

LET NO FEELING of discouragement prey upon you and in the end you are sure to succeed.

ABRAHAM LINCOLN

WORDS OF encouragement fan the spark of genius into the flame of achievement.

WILFERD A. PETERSON

YOU ARE VALUABLE... not because of what you do or what you have done, but simply because you are.

ANONYMOUS

You Are Blessed

How are we rewarded? Do we receive blessings by doing nothing? Do you always know why you feel blessed?

Often times, we measure rewards in our life by the things that we do. But are the things that we do actions of obedience—following what we are supposed to do in order to receive something in return? When growing up, you probably heard the saying, "if you are good, then good things will happen to you." Meaning, "be obedient and you will be blessed."

But, we don't always know why blessings come our way. It may be due to a good deed, obedience, or a number of other reasons. What about the times when you intentionally obey and do the right things and you didn't receive a blessing (or feel blessed)? It's easy to get caught up in trying to figure out "the why and why not."

When you follow what you feel is right and best, the results are beneficial and blessings in your life.

TIMELESS WISDOM

Remember, when you do the right thing, even if you don't receive a direct blessing from it, it will feel like you did.

THE GREATEST GOOD you can do for another is not just to share your riches, but to reveal to him his own.

BENJAMIN DISRAELI

NO MATTER how busy you are, you must take time to make the other person important.

MARY KAY ASH

THE BEST WAY to cheer yourself up is to cheer everybody else up.

MARK TWAIN

MOST OF THE THINGS worth doing in the world had been declared impossible before they were done.

ANONYMOUS

Promise of Today... Hope for Tomorrow

Make no mistake about it, thoughts are powerful things. Your thoughts have the power to lift you or to hold you down. When you acquire the habit of hopeful thinking, you will have acquired a powerful tool for empowering your life.

So if you fall into the habit of negative thinking, think again. The promise of today can only be achieved through a strong sense of hope for tomorrow and beyond. If we let negative thoughts control our thinking, then the consistency of hope will diminish and create doubt and even despair.

Live for today, but hold your hands open to tomorrow. Anticipate the future and its changes with optimism. Remember, there is a seed of hope in every event, every circumstance, and every unpleasant situation in which you may find yourself.

Develop a pattern of thinking that allows
you to embrace the promises of today
while looking forward to the hope of
tomorrow.

SOW SEEDS of hope and enjoy optimism.
Sow seeds of doubt and expect insecurity.

MAX LUCADO

HOPE NEVER DIES where faith is strong,
and faith grows strong in the presence of hope.

CHAD WITMEYER

WHEN THERE IS no hope in the future
there is no power in the present.

JOHN MAXWELL

OPTIMISM is the faith that leads to achievement.
Nothing can be done without hope and
confidence.

HELEN KELLER

Attitude is
Everything

DO YOU EVER WONDER how positive people stay so upbeat? You know the ones I'm referring to. They brighten rooms just by walking in. No matter what challenges they may be facing, they give you the same hospitality you expect to receive while visiting a tropical resort. Everybody wants to be around them.

By nature, we prefer positive people because it's no fun spending time with a negative person. Most of us aspire to be positive people. It's advantageous to an optimistic, positive outlook

For positive, optimistic people, life seems to come easier. Doors of opportunity open more frequently. They make friends, earn respect, close deals and gain loyalty and trust from others. People enjoy them and want to be like them.

How can we emulate that? What does it take for us to have a positive attitude? Good news! To increase your outlook, always remember that attitudes are contagious. Ask yourself, "Is mine worth catching?"

Search out people who will challenge you, believe in you and inspire you to improve. No matter what's going on in your life, another person can help you shoot higher, laugh louder, and look forward to tomorrow. Our very lives change when we have positive, loving friends with whom we can share our victories and defeats.

To create a life (and person) you desire to become, your attitude—both inward and outward—will help establish the person you will become.

Attitudes determine actions. You are not what you think you are. What you think, you are.

A Winning Attitude

Success is mainly a question of attitude. If you go into an undertaking expecting to succeed, the odds are great that you'll succeed. If you go in fearful of losing, you're more likely to lose.

If two evenly matched teams clash in competition, which team is more likely to win? In all likelihood, the team with a winning tradition is victorious. That's because its coaches and players have a mindset to win. And the competition knows it. On the other hand, if a team has a losing tradition, its players are often surprised by victory, which is why they have mediocre seasons even when talent isn't in question.

It's been said that the late Bear Bryant, legendary football coach of the University of Alabama, went into each game with a winning attitude that was worth at least one touchdown for the Crimson Tide.

TIMELESS WISDOM

Cultivate a winning attitude. It will sustain you even when the odds seem stacked against you.

A GREAT ATTITUDE is not the result of success; success is the result of a great attitude

EARL NIGHTINGALE

ABILITY IS what you're capable of doing. Motivation determines what you do. Attitude determines how well you do it.

RAYMOND CHANDLER

WE HAVE A RIGHT to choose our attitude.

VIKTOR FRANKL

THE MESSAGE IS CLEAR: Plan with attitude, prepare with aptitude, participate with servitude, receive with gratitude, and this should be enough to separate you from the multitudes.

KRISH DHANAM

Be Strong and Believe

As you take the next few steps in life's journey, you will be tested along the way. Life is a series of successes and failures, celebrations and disappointments, joys and sorrows. For every step along the way, through every triumph and disappointment, dig deeply to find your inner strength to carry you through.

Even in triumph, it's tempting to shift the focus to "it's all about me" versus all the factors that brought a positive result. And when challenges become an issue, we tend to blame other things and/or people. Or we run from the issue instead of directly taking it on, confronting it, and bringing a resolution.

No matter the situation or the outcome, in the end, it's important that you remain strong and hold to what you believe is right and best. Building the right value system will enable you to stay aligned in your beliefs. Your beliefs serve as a strong foundation for how you stay focused and anchored in your life.

Today and every day, make sure you stand strong in your beliefs. You have big plans to achieve much. Rely on your knowledge that a strong foundation is important to your journey through all life's situations—positive or negative.

TIMELESS WISDOM

You cannot see the future so let your instincts, beliefs, and actions be the guiding factors along life's journey.

MANY PEOPLE limit themselves to what they think they can do. You can go as far as your mind lets you. What you believe, remember, you can achieve.

MARY KAY ASH

ALL THE WONDERS you seek are within yourself.

THOMAS BROWN

YOUR SUCCESS depends mainly upon what you think of yourself and whether you believe in yourself. You can succeed if nobody else believes it; but will never succeed if you don't' believe in yourself.

WILLIAM J.H. BOETCKER

The Choice is Yours

Your life is a series of choices. From the instant you wake up until the moment you hit the pillow, you make a lot of decisions. Decisions about the things you do, decisions about the words you speak, and decisions about the thoughts you choose to think. Simply put, the quality of those decisions determines the quality of your life.

So, if you sincerely want to lead a life that pleases you and that meets your expectations, then you must make choices that are sometimes difficult and not always popular or appealing to your friends and following.

In the end, choices come down to what you decide. Decisions help mold and shape you. There is learning in every choice we make. There are results in every decision we make. What life lessons and outcomes do you hope to achieve through the choices and decisions that you will make? You have time to think it through. Don't worry; life gives "grace points" of learning and second chance opportunities.

TIMELESS WISDOM

First you make choices... and pretty soon those choices begin to shape your life. That's why you must make smart choices... or face the consequences of making dumb ones.

THE ONLY TRUE freedom each of us has in life is the freedom to choose. The most important choice is who we will become.

JOHN MAXWELL

LIFE CHOOSES different paths for us to follow. We choose which one to take.

ANONYMOUS

NO MATTER WHAT, your attitude is a choice. Circumstances may not be of your choosing but your attitude is all yours.

MAC ANDERSON

IN A MOMENT of decision the best thing you can do is the right thing. The worst thing you can do is nothing.

THEODORE ROOSEVELT

In Times of Adversity

Have you experienced any recent setbacks in your life? If so, explore the situation and seek out the life lesson as a teaching tool. Instead of complaining about life's sad state of happenings, learn what needs to learned, change what needs to be changed, and move on.

View failure as an opportunity to reassess your life. View life's inevitable disappointments as opportunities to learn more about yourself and your world. Life can be and will be difficult at times. And everybody will make mistakes. Your job is to make them only once or at least minimize them to the lesser degree.

There is a common saying, "in the midst of difficulty lies the opportunity." Possibly your most challenging times will prove to be the most opportunistic times to achieve breakthrough results.

TIMELESS WISDOM

When you make a mistake, the time to make things better is now, not later. The sooner you address your challenge, the better. Don't let it become a larger issue.

ALL THINGS are difficult before they are easy.

JOHN NORLEY

ADVERSITY is the first path to truth.

GEORGE GORDON BYRON

FAILURE is not fatal, but failure to change might be.

JOHN WOODEN

I CAN ACCEPT failure. Everyone fails at something. But I can't accept not trying

MICHAEL JORDAN

Remember to Laugh

Laughter is often times the best remedy for having a bad day or getting through a stressful moment. Because of inevitable things we encounter and deal with on a daily basis, laughter can become a distant memory. We have reasons for the need to be cheerful and many times laughter becomes a result.

No one wants to be in a grumpy mood. No one likes to be around someone who is a grouch. Life seems to flow better when you're happy and you're laughing a little more each day.

Today as you go about your daily activities, approach life with a grin and even a chuckle. After all, laughter was created for a reason. So just laugh!

TIMELESS WISDOM

Learn to laugh. Life has a light side—look for it. Often life is trying to get your attention especially when times are tough. Laughter is medicine for the soul, so take your medicine early and often

LAUGHTER is to the soul what soap is to the body.

MAC ANDERSON

THE HUMAN RACE has only one really effective weapon and that is laughter. The moment it arises, all your irritations and resentments slip away, and the sunny spirit takes their place.

MARK TWAIN

LAUGHTER is the best medicine for a long and happy life. He who laughs—lasts!

WILFERD A. PETERSON

LAUGHTER is a tranquilizer with no side effects.

ARNOLD H. GLASOW

More Complaints?

Because we are imperfect human beings, we often lose sight of our blessings. Ironically, most of us have more blessings that we can count, but we may still find reasons to complain about the minor frustrations of everyday life. To do so, of course, is not only wrong, but it is also shortsighted and limits our ability to identity potentials in ourselves.

What type of person are you? Are you easily tempted to complain about the daily frustrations of your life?

Today, try to make it a practice to be thankful and count your blessings, not your hardships. It's a better way to live, and you'll be glad you did.

TIMELESS WISDOM

If you're wise, fill yourself with gratitude. When you do, there's simply no room left for complaints.

GRATITUDE conserves the vital energies of a person more than any other attitude tested.

HANS SELYE

I AM GRATEFUL for all of my problems. After each one was overcome, I became stronger and more able to meet those that were still to come. I grew in all my difficulties.

J.C. PENNEY

REAL OPTIMISM is aware of problems but recognizes solutions; knows about difficulties but believes they can be overcome; sees the negatives, but accentuates the positives; is exposed to the worst but expects the best; has reason to complain, but chooses to smile.

WILLIAM ARTHUR WARD

A WINNER is big enough to admit his mistakes, smart enough to profit from them, and strong enough to correct them.

JOHN MAXWELL

Good Pressures, Bad Pressures

As you have figured out by now, life is filled with pressures—some good and some bad. And both kinds cause different responses and reactions.

The pressures you encountered and experienced thus far are a direct result of encounters—school work, team competition, friends and family, work of various levels, time management, and the general responsibilities of daily living—either bringing good or bad pressure to light.

Society seeks to drive certain pressures faster than we often times care and/or want. We have the power to control and manage how the pressures affect our response to them and, more importantly, how that impacts ourselves. Possibly it's as simple as the choices we make, the friends we choose, and the situations we place ourselves in.

Pressures can be good or bad. Obviously, the more you seek out and experience the good, the less you have to deal with how you are going to deal with the bad.

YOU CAN make your life whatever you want it to be.

WALLY AMOS

PRESSURE causes some people to break; others to break records.

WILLIAM ARTHUR WARD

WHEN THE GOING gets tough, those with a dream keep going.

BEN FELDMAN

Your Core...
Your Integrity

HAVING A CLEAR PICTURE of who we are and what we want is something most of us don't think about. We start and end our days without giving much thought to whether or not we are on the intended path we should be on. Most of us lead our lives without giving much thought to our true purpose or intentions. We end up trying to live the lives that marketing and advertising companies misguide us into believing we should be living.

The end result is a society of people that are out of balance and out of touch with what really matters to them and to others. We spend so much time trying to be something and someone other than who we really are.

Setting goals regarding where you want to get in life or who you want to be is a good start. And if you don't begin with who you are and where you are, it will be difficult to set a course for your desired outcome. You must begin by looking inward to understand who you are and what your core values and beliefs are. Only then will you be able to chart a course to the life you deserve.

Try these action steps:

Give yourself a check-up from the neck up.

Write down your core values and beliefs.

Share them with your friends and family.

Ask yourself if you are living a life consistent with these values and beliefs.

Create a picture in your mind of what you want, and who you want to be in your life.

Live the vision.

Set clear goals that are consistent with your values and beliefs.

Celebrate your accomplishments.

Acknowledge and be thankful for everything for which you feel you should be grateful.

A Life of Integrity

Integrity is built slowly over a lifetime. It is a key "core value"—difficult to build but easy to tear down. Like most values, integrity is built over time through a process of consistency and gaining trust.

Striving for integrity, we must seek to live each day with intentional discipline through honesty, and ethics. When we do, at least two things happen:

Integrity becomes a habit, and

People begin to believe and trust that our practices reflect our intention.

Living a life of integrity isn't always the easiest way or necessarily the popular choice based on society's defined values. But it's the right way and, if desired it should be your way too.

TIMELESS WISDOM

The real test of integrity is being willing to tell the truth when it's hard and own up to it even if it's not directly pointing back to you. What does it look like to you when stepping up isn't the popular choice even it doesn't make you look bad?

IF YOU HAVE INTEGRITY, nothing else matters. If you don't have integrity, nothing else matters.

ALAN K. SIMPSON

INTEGRITY is the first step to true greatness. Men love to praise, but are slow to practice it. Maintain it in high places costs self-denial. In all places it is liable to opposition, but its end is glorious.

CHARLES SIMMONS

INTEGRITY is one of several paths. It distinguishes itself from the others because it is the right path and the only one on which you never get lost.

M.H. MCKEE

Nothing But the Truth

One of the early writers on wisdom advised, "Never support an experience which does not support your beliefs as its source." These words serve as a powerful reminder that we are to walk, think, and talk in terms of ultimate truth.

But, we live in a world that presents us with countless lies that distract us from a foundation of solid truth. These lies and low moral issues have the potential to erode truthful intentions. Greed, jealously and envy can lead us into dishonesty with ourselves and with others.

Dishonesty is a habit. Once we start bending the truth, we're likely to keep bending it. A far better strategy is to acquire the habit of being completely honest with others and with ourselves.

Honesty is also a habit—a habit that pays powerful dividends for those who place character above convenience. So, the next time you're tempted to bend the truth—or to break it—ask yourself this simple question: "Are you acting on the truth or trying to define your own interpretation of what you think the truth is, or should be?"

TIMELESS WISDOM

Listen carefully to your conscience. When you do, your actions will be honorable and your character will take care of itself. It's the thoughts of the heart that shape a person's life.

DON'T WORRY so much about your self-esteem. Worry more about your character. Integrity is its own reward.

DR. LAURA SCHLESSINGER

SOCIETY IS BUILT upon trust and trust upon confidence in one another's integrity.

ROBERT SOUTH

IT'S NOT the things we get, but the hearts we touch, that will measure our success in life.

ANONYMOUS

NEVER LOSE SIGHT of the fact that the most important yardstick of your success will be how you treat other people.

BARBARA BUSH

For the Love of Money

As a society we are in love with money and the things that money can buy. But what about the things that money can't buy? We've heard the marketing claim, "priceless!" What you may classify as "priceless" may not be what the person next to you does.

Today, we place too much emphasis on possessions and not enough on people, felt needs, emotions, and other "valued intangibles" that, frankly, money can't buy. We must, to the best of our ability, love our neighbors—including those closest to us—as ourselves, and we must, to the best of our abilities, resist the temptation to place possessions ahead of what we value most.

Money, in and of itself, should not be an inhibitor but rather a contributor to both our needs and wants. But when money gets in the way of important "life values," it is then when money becomes a limited liability. And if money becomes your prized possession, then maybe it's time for you to find a way to bless someone else through giving. The amount of giving is not the point. However, the actual act of giving to someone or something else provides a bigger blessing for you.

When you realize that this world is not all about generating financial gain to satisfy your wants, your outlook on how you spend your money begins to change.

SUCCESS IS FINDING, or making, that position which enables you to contribute to the world the very greatest services of which you are capable.... Success consists of being and doing, not simply accumulating.

B.C. FORBES

REAL GENEROSITY is doing something nice for someone who will never find out.

FRANK A. CLARK

DON'T BE RELUCTANT to give of yourself generously; it's the mark of caring and compassion and personal greatness.

BRIAN TRACY

THAT'S WHAT I consider true generosity. You give your all and yet you always feel as if it costs you nothing.

SIMONE DE BEAUVOIR

Fit to Serve

In today's society, leisure is glorified and consumption is commercialized. Be careful that your life is not consumed with gluttony or laziness. Rather stay sharp, full of energy and ready to contribute. There are great things to accomplish and there are plenty of ways to serve in order to create a greater cause and effect.

By design, we are equipped with certain abilities to obtain and make things happen. Even if you don't have all the physical abilities, life offers a plethora of ways to serve various needs. Live with an expectation of "I'm ready to do my fair share of work to accomplish the task."

Given that there are so many distractions and temptations, you may find it all too easy to make unhealthy choices. Your challenge, of course, is to resist these kinds of temptations by every means you can.

TIMELESS WISDOM

Simply put, it's up to you to assume the ultimate responsibility for your health and well-being—to be ready to serve at a moment's notice or even a planned moment. Are you prepared for the right opportunity to serve and help make a difference?

BE WISE in the use of time.
The question is not, How much time have we?
The question is, what shall we do with it?

ANNA ROBERTSON BROWN

TODAY IS YOUR DAY and mine, the only day we have, the day in which we play our part. What our part may signify in the great whole we may not understand; but we are here to play it, and now is our time.

DAVID STARR JORDAN

WE ARE NOT living in eternity. We have only this moment, sparkling like a star in our hand—and melting like a snowflake. Let us use it before it is too late.

MARIE BEYNON RAY

Actions that Reflect Our Values

Our journey in life will help us shape our actions. We continue to learn that our actions are accurate reflections of our values. In short, we should be practical in our values and quick to act whenever we see an opportunity to respond in a way that aligns with our values.

Are you the kind of person who is practical and willing to dig in and do whatever needs to be done when it needs to be done? If so, congratulations! The results of your actions will acknowledge your service and reward it. But if you find yourself more interested in the fine points of "you" rather than seeing the needs and opportunities around you, it's time to rearrange your priorities.

The world needs value-driven people to roll up their sleeves and engage in initiatives that reflect and generate results that have impact globally and locally. Vision is effective when followed with action. The two combined create a powerful effect.

Because actions do speak louder than words, it's always a good time to let your actions speak for themselves.

MAKE THE MOST of yourself, for that is all there is of you.

RALPH WALDO EMERSON

ACTION conquers fear.

PETE ZARLENGA

DISCIPLINE is the habit of taking consistent action until one can perform with unconscious competence.

JHOON RHEE

CHOP YOUR OWN wood and it will warm you twice.

HENRY FORD

Honesty, the Best Policy

From the time we are children, we are taught that honesty is the best policy, but sometimes, being honest is hard. So, we convince ourselves that it's alright to tell 'little white lies." However, there's a problem. Little white lies tend to grow up and cause complicated issues in our lives.

If you're striving for the best policy, then the issue of honesty is not a topic for debate. Honesty is not just the best policy, it's the only policy. And if the best policy is truly what we're seeking then we must avoid all lies—small or otherwise.

If you're tempted to sow the seeds of deception (perhaps in the form of a 'harmless" white lie) resist that temptation.

TIMELESS WISDOM

Beware of telling "white" lies. Sometimes, we're tempted to 'shade" the truth. Unfortunately, little white lies have a tendency to turn dark and grow much bigger. The best strategy is to avoid untruths of all sizes and colors.

WE CANNOT become what we need to be by remaining what we are.

MAX DE PREE

YOU CAN'T BUILD a reputation on what you're going to do.

HENRY FORD

SEEK TO DO GOOD and you will find that honesty will run after you.

JAMES FREEMAN CLARKE

YOU CAN'T TALK YOURSELF out of a problem you behave yourself into.

STEPHEN COVEY

No Is An Answer

How many times do we find ourselves saying "yes" when we should have just answered "no?" Too often it is easy to just say "I will do it" without properly processing the request to best determine if it is beneficial to you or to the situation. What may sound good at the time doesn't always mean "good" later.

What about when we really want something? It's even easier to "yes." Our judgment can be clouded and what seems to be "an easy yes" turns into a potentially bad decision. "No" would have been a better choice.

We cannot always know the plan—even if it seems to be a good or right plan for us. However, our intuition and experience will help us to direct our choices to make the best and right decisions.

TIMELESS WISDOM

When our conscience says "no," that is a good thing. Listen to yourself. Trust and lead yourself when choosing between answering "yes" and "no." Lean on others to help you especially when you begin to doubt the decision you are about to make.

TRUE GRIT is making a decision and standing by it, doing what must be done.

JOHN WAYNE

A LEADER, once convinced a particular course of action is the right one, must have the determination to stick with it and be undaunted when the going gets rough.

RONALD REAGAN

A TRUE LEADER has the confidence to stand alone, the courage to make tough decisions and the compassion to listen to the needs of others. They are much like eagles...They don't flock, you find them one at a time.

M.H. MCKEE

Authentic
Character

CHARACTER is the real foundation of all worthwhile success. A good question to ask yourself is, "What kind of world would it be if everybody were just like me?" Never be ashamed of doing what is right. And never esteem anything that goes against your character.

You do not have to or need to say, "I will be bad." You only have to say, "I will not choose the best choice," and the evidence of a damaged reputation is already settled. There is no such thing as a necessary evil. Phillips Brooks said, "A man who lives right and is right has more power in his silence than another has by his words."

A person's reputation may not recognize their character if they met in the dark. To shape your character, you must begin at the control center—your heart. Personal bankruptcy is inevitable when a man is no longer able to keep the interest paid on his moral obligations.

Live so that your friends can defend you, but never have to do so. Consider what Woodrow Wilson said, "If you will think about what you ought to do for other people, your character will take care of itself." Excellence in character is shown by doing with no one seeing what we would be doing with the whole world watching.

It's hard to climb high when your character is low. The world's shortest and best speech is said by the traffic sign: Keep Right.

Character Counts

Character is built slowly over a lifetime. It is the sum of every right decision, every honest word, every noble thought, and every heartfelt sentiment. It is forged on the anvil of honorable works and polished by the twin virtues of generosity and humility. Character is a precious thing—difficult to build but easy to tear down.

If you strive to gain character, seek to live each day with discipline, honesty, and belief. When we do, integrity becomes a best practice. Integrity is the glue that holds our way of life together.

We must constantly strive to keep our integrity intact. When wealth is lost, nothing is lost. When health is lost, something is lost. When character is lost, all is lost.

Take time to think about your own character,
both your strong points and your weaknesses.
Then list three aspects of your character—
longstanding habits or troublesome behaviors—
that you would like to change. Finally,
take steps to improve yourself and your life.

CHARACTER is not in the mind; it is in the will.

FULTON J. SHEEN

OUR WORDS reveal our thoughts; our manners
mirror our self-esteem; our actions reflect our
character; our habits predict the future.

WILLIAM ARTHUR WARD

WEAKNESS of attitude becomes a weakness
of character.

ALBERT EINSTEIN

CHARACTER is the total of thousands of small
daily strivings to live up to the best that in in us.

LT. GEN. ARTHUR TRUDEAU

Measure and Manage Your Words

Media and social media reminds us daily that "reckless words pierce like a sword, but the tongue of the wise brings healing." (from Proverbs 12:18). If you seek to be a source of encouragement to others, then you must measure your words carefully. And that's a tall order given that often times it is difficult to carry out.

Today, make this promise to yourself: vow to be an honest, effective, encouraging communicator to those around you—in the workplace, your home, and everyplace in between. Communicate wisely, not impulsively. Use words of kindness and praise, not words of anger or dissension.

Learn how to be truthful without being cruel. Remember that you have the power to heal others or to injure them, to lift others up or to hold them back. And when you learn how to lift them up, you'll soon discover that you've lifted yourself up too.

Try being a brief communicator. Longwinded monologues, although satisfying to the speaker, are usually torture to the listener. So when in doubt, say less and listen more.

TRUST YOURSELF. Think for yourself. Act for yourself. Speak for yourself. Be yourself.

MARVA COLLINS

THE ABILITY to simplify means to eliminate the unnecessary so that the necessary may speak.

HANS HOFMANN

WHAT ANOTHER would have done as well as you, do not do it. What another would have said as well as you, do not say it. What another would have written as well, do not write it. Be faithful to that which exists nowhere but in yourself.

ANDRE GIDE

Excellence, Not Excuses

Excuses are everywhere...excellence is not. If you seek excellence, you must avoid the bad habit of making excuses.

Whatever your job description, it's up to you, and no one else, to become, "a master of your craft." It's up to you to do your job right—and to do it right now. When you do, you'll discover that excellence is its own reward... but not its only reward.

Few things in life fire up a person's commitment like dedication to excellence. While it's not easy to achieve, it should be the bulls-eye that we're trying to hit. If we strive to hit dead center, we have a better chance to achieve a greater shot of excellence than just throwing at the target.

TIMELESS WISDOM

Today, think of something important that you've been putting off. Then think if you used excuses to avoid the responsibility. Finally, ask yourself what you can do today to finish the work you've been avoiding.

GUARD WELL your spare moments. They are like uncut diamonds. Discard them and their value will never be known. Improve them and they will become the brightest gems in a useful life.

RALPH WALDO EMERSON

TIME IS EVERYTHING. Anything you want, anything you accomplish—pleasure, success, fortune—is measured in time.

JOYCE C. HALL

IN TRUTH, people can generally make time for what they choose to do; it is not really the time but the will that is lacking.

SIR JOHN LUBBOCK

A Positive Influence

What kind of example am I? The answer to that question determines, in large part, whether or not we are positive influences on our own little corners of the world.

Are you the kind of person whose life serves as a role model? Are you a person whose behavior serves as a powerful example for you and others? Are you the type of person whose actions, day in and day out, are based upon integrity and ethics?

If so, you are not only heading in the right direction, you are also a powerful force for good in a world that desperately needs positive influences such as yours.

TIMELESS WISDOM

The most important way you can influence others is how you direct your own life. To influence, you must know how to be an influencer and build trust and loyalty through a set of shared values.

THOSE WHO BRING sunshine into the lives of others cannot keep it from themselves.

JAMES M. BARRIE

A SUCCESSFUL MAN is one who can't count the number of other successful people he helped to the top.

ORLANDO A. BATTISTA

SUCCESS has nothing to do with what you gain in life or accomplish for yourself. It's what you do for others that matters most.

DANNY THOMAS

SOMETIMES our candle goes out, but is blown into flame by an encounter with another human being.

ALBERT SCHWEITZER

Dealing with Disappointment

From time to time, all of us face life-altering disappointments that leave us breathless. Oftentimes, these disappointments come unexpectedly, leaving us with more questions than answers. But even when we don't have all the answers—or, for that matter, none of the answers—it's okay.

When we reach these times, it's good to hit the "refresh" button and begin to think clearly and walk through a step by step process with the goal of dealing with and solving the issue.

Whatever our circumstances, whether we stand atop the highest mountain or wander through the darkest valley, our only task is to walk through, sometimes leaning on others, seeking wisdom, and pursuing answers. But be careful not to create a "sooner than later" expectation of how to deal with your disappointment.

It can create undo stress, anxiety, and, in the end, more disappointment.

TIMELESS WISDOM

You can increase your supply of courage by sharing it. Courage to walk through disappointment is contagious. Courage inspired by a strong trust in relying on other people, your beliefs, and other means can fuel a wave of breakthrough like no other. Today, as you interact with friends, family, and others share your courage, your hopes, your dreams, and your enthusiasm. It could become as big a blessing to them as it is to you.

COURAGE is not limited to the battlefield. The real tests of courage are much quieter. They are the inner tests, like enduring pain when the room is empty or standing alone when you're misunderstood.

CHARLES SWINDOLL

COURAGE is the decision to place your dreams above your fears.

ANONYMOUS

COURAGE is resistance to fear, mastery of fear—not absence of fear.

MARK TWAIN

A GREAT LEADER'S courage to fulfill his vision comes from passion, not position.

JOHN MAXWELL

Mentoring Moments

Here's a simple, yet effective way to strengthen your opportunity to learn from others. Choose role models that you look up to and that have a consistent pattern in how they conduct their life.

Emulate like-minded people or those who you aspire to be. Seek out mentors who by their words, presence, and actions make you a better person.

If nothing else, as a gift to yourself, select, from your friends and family, a mentor whose judgment you trust. Then listen carefully to your mentor's advice and be willing to accept their advice, even if accepting it requires effort to the point of stretching you to new levels of intentional growth.

TIMELESS WISDOM

When it comes to mentors, you need them. When it comes to mentoring, they need you.

TRAINING teaches people what to do; education teaches people what to be.

NIDO R. QUBEIN

THE DOORS OF WISDOM are never shut.

BEN FRANKLIN

ADVICE IS LIKE SNOW—the softer it falls, the longer it dwells upon, and the deeper it sinks into the mind.

SAMUEL TAYLOR COLERIDGE

THE YOUNG do not follow our preachings— they follow us.

ROBERT BRAULT

Temporary Setbacks

The occasional disappointments and failures of life are inevitable. Such setbacks are simply the price that we must occasionally pay for our willingness to take risks as we follow our dreams. But even when we encounter bitter disappointments, we must never lose our will to persevere.

When we do encounter inevitable difficulties, are we set up to handle such challenges or do we fail? But why do we fail? Is it because we have not properly sustained ourselves to handle the setback?

Let's face it, setbacks are emotional, and can be physically draining and unfortunately can last longer than we want or had hoped. No matter the duration of the setback, the goal is to not only to get past it but more importantly, summon the strength to get through it.

Don't let temporary setbacks turn into long term or life-long durations. Learn how to build the sustainable factors to get you through them and to make them as brief as possible.

TIMELESS WISDOM

Use your experiences—both good and bad—to learn, to grow, to share, and to teach. These become sustainable factors to handle future setbacks—big or small, temporary or otherwise.

PROBLEMS are nothing but wake up calls for creativity.

GERHARD GSCHWANDTNER

IT'S THE CONSTANT and determined effort that breaks down all resistance, sweeps away all obstacles.

CLAUDE M. BRISTOL

LIFE IS AN ECHO; what you send out comes back.

CHINESE PROVERB

EVERY CRUCIAL EXPERIENCE can be regarded as a setback—or the start of a new kind of development.

MARY ROBERTS RINEHART

Building Self-Esteem

Would you like to make the world a better place and feel better about yourself at the same time? If so, you can start by practicing the Golden Rule—treat other people with respect, kindness, courtesy, and love. When we do, we make other people happy and we feel better about ourselves.

If you're wondering how to make the world—and your world—a better place, here's a great place to start: let the Golden Rule be your rule. And if you want to know how to treat other people, ask the person you see every time you look in the mirror.

Our self-esteem produces confidence and motivates us in ways that build. It benefits not only ourselves but, more importantly, it does good for the people around us. You can't do good for others unless you have the proper levels of self-worth and pride in your own life.

TIMELESS WISDOM

The more you help others, the better you'll feel about yourself. So don't delay. Somebody needs your help today.

GIVE TO THE WORLD the best you have and the best will come back to you.

MADELINE BRIDGES

WE HAVE COMMITTED the Golden Rule to memory; let us now commit it to life.

EDWIN MARKHAM

A MAN wrapped up in himself makes a very small bundle.

BENJAMIN FRANKLIN

YOU CAN HAVE anything you want in life if you will just help enough other people get what they want.

ZIG ZIGLAR

At Peace with Your Purpose

Everywhere we turn, or so it seems, the world promises fulfillment, contentment, and happiness. But the view that the world offers seems to vanish and it is often incomplete.

Sometimes, amid the overwhelming busyness of our daily lives, we can forfeit our happiness—whether temporary or otherwise—to things that offer short-term pleasure versus long term joy.

Yet, we may have to wrestle with the "here and now" versus being at peace with our purpose based on our personal vision, goals, and values.

Don't let your purpose in life be replaced with substitutes that take away your peace in knowing who you are and what you want to accomplish. Seek the kind of fulfillment that drives you to greater purpose. When this happens, peace will automatically take over.

TIMELESS WISDOM

If you want to increase your sense of fulfillment, strive to find that path for your life...and follow it.

PURPOSE and laughter are the twins that must not separate. Each is empty without the other.

ROBERT K. GREENLEAF

THREE GRAND ESSENTIALS to happiness in this life are something to do, something to love, and something to hope for.

JOSEPH ADDISON

WE ACT AS THOUGH comfort and luxury were the chief requirements of life, when all that we need to make us really happy is something to be enthusiastic about.

CHARLES KINGSLEY

LIFE IS MADE of memorable moments. We must teach ourselves to really live... to love the journey not destination.

ANNA QUINDLEN

Aim High and Take Chances

ALL THE GREAT DISCOVERIES have been made by people with great vision. Significant achievements have never been obtained by taking small risks on unimportant issues. Do not waste time planning, analyzing and risking on small ideas. It is always wise to spend more time on decisions that are irreversible and less on those that are reversible.

Learn to stretch and reach way out. Aim high and take chances. Average people only look to next year based on last year. Instead, reach for the potential, don't just plan based on the past. How can you drive where you want to go, if you're looking in the rear view mirror?

Those who make great strides take chances and plan past the challenges of life.

Almost nothing in life is more frustrating than becoming really good at unimportant tasks. Don't get so caught up in the small matters that you can't take advantage of important opportunities. Most people spend their entire lives lowering buckets into empty wells and then waste their days trying to pull them up again and again.

Choose to dream big; strive to reach the full potential of your life. Choose to focus on the important issues of life, not the insignificant.

Security and opportunity are total strangers. If an undertaking does not include risk, it is not worthy of being called a real dream. A famous old saying goes like this, "Even a turtle doesn't get ahead unless he sticks his neck out." Dream big, there's really no other way to live!

Taking Risks

As we consider the uncertainties of the future, we are confronted with a powerful temptation— the temptation to "play it safe." Unwilling to move mountains, we complain about the road bumps along the path. Unwilling to entertain great hopes for your life, even the next week, day, even minutes, you focus on the unfairness of today. Unwilling to have trust or trust in the key things (and people) in your life can cause you to side-step and miss out on the giant leaps.

Today, seek out courage to step beyond the boundaries of your doubts. Ask others to come alongside you and help guide you to realizing your full potential—allowing you to be freed from the fear of failure. This doesn't mean a "safe" place but rather the "right" place. Remember, those two places are seldom the same.

Often times, the first step in taking the risk is deciding to do it. After the decision is made, it becomes easier to walk out the next steps to determine the level of the risk and its opportunity. It's almost impossible to know how much of a risk it is until you know the level of opportunity and its cost.

TIMELESS WISDOM

If you're about to make a big decision or take a significant risk, first get advice from people you trust and value their insight. And the bigger the decision, more reason to take the right steps toward making the right one.

PROGRESS always involves risks. You can't steal second base and keep your foot on first.

FREDERICK B. WILCOX

DON'T BE AFRAID to go out on a limb... that's where the fruit is.

HARRY S. TRUMAN

YOU WIN A FEW, you lose a few. Some get rained out. But you got to dress for all of them.

LEROY "SATCHEL" PAIGE

WE CANNOT GET what we've never had, unless we're willing to do what we've never done.

BRIAN TRACY

The World and You

We live in the world, but we must be careful to not conform to things of the world that don't align with how we want to live. We must put our priorities first and everything else second. But because we are imperfect in nature, we can easily be tempted to do otherwise.

The 21st-century world is noisy and fast paced, filled with countless opportunities to be distracted. The disguises of the world seem to communicate, "Give me your time, your money, your energy, and your thoughts!" While the world needs our attention, it should be on our time and at our decision.

It's easy to let the world dictate what we do rather than that which best meets our needs and even our wants.

TIMELESS WISDOM

The world's power to distract and detour is like rush hour traffic. Thankfully, we have the right to make decisions that steer us clear of on-coming distractions.

OUR GREATEST DANGER in life is in permitting the urgent things to crowd out the important.

CHARLES HUMMEL

I THINK WE ALL HAVE a little voice inside us that will guide us if we shut out all the noise and clutter from our lives and listen to that voice. It will tell us the right thing to do.

CHRISTOPHER REEVE

AGAIN AND AGAIN, the impossible problem
is solved when we see that the problem is only
a tough decision waiting to be made.

ROBERT H. SCHULLER

Recouping Your Losses

Have you ever made a financial blunder?
Lost something of worth? Or you had to sell
something in order to pay for something else?
Almost everyone experiences some type of
financial pressure from time to time, and if you
have not already, perhaps you will.

When we commit the inevitable missteps in life,
we must correct them, learn from them, and
apply wisdom and best practices not to repeat
them. Then our mistakes become lessons, and
our lives become adventures in growth, not life
in "the norm."

So here's the big question: Have you used
your mistakes as stumbling blocks or stepping
stones? The answer to that question will
determine how quickly you gain financial
security and peace of mind.

Live within your means and save money from every paycheck. Never spend more than you make.

REMEMBER, the free cheese is in a mousetrap.

ANONYMOUS

A BUDGET is telling your money where to go instead of wondering where it went.

JOHN MAXWELL

THE PRICE OF GREATNESS is responsibility.

WINSTON CHURCHILL

PERSONAL FINANCE is 80 percent behavior and only 20 percent head knowledge.

DAVE RAMSEY

The Journey Ahead...
Seven Steps to Success

As you progress along the journey, reflect on what got you to this point. What were the key factors? Now, begin to look ahead. What do you envision? It's a day to day, walk-before-you-run, process of learning and living to find that stride in life that helps you manage and maximize the everyday pace.

It's going to be an incredible journey! Sometimes you will experience excitement; other times, only discipline will carry you through. But always remember, success is waiting for you to make the first move.

Get started by making these seven steps best practice guidelines to developing a successful journey.

STEP 1

Commit to personal growth.

One of the greatest mistakes you make is to have the wrong focus. Success doesn't come from acquiring, achieving, or advancing. It comes only as the result of growing. If you make it your goal to grow, you will begin to see positive results in your life.

STEP 2

Value the process more than the destination.

Specific life events are good for making decisions, but it's the process of change and growth that has lasting value. If you want to go on to the next level, strive for continual improvement.

STEP 3

Don't wait for the days you feel good.

There is an old saying, "You can get more done in life if you only work on the days when you feel good." The further you push yourself, the farther you'll go. Motivate yourself to achieve life's best, regardless of how you feel on a given day. To be successful, you must persevere.

STEP 4

Be willing to sacrifice your wants for opportunities.

There are many "opportunity costs" that life presents. But in reality, for everything in life, you pay a price. You choose to pay it on the front end or the back end. If you pay first, then you will enjoy greater rewards in the end.

Dream big.

It doesn't pay to dream small. In the book, *If It Ain't Broke, Break It*, authors Robert J. Kriegel and Louis Patler didn't have a clue as to what people's limits are. "All the tests, stopwatches, and finish lines in the world can't measure human potential," stated Patler. When pursuing your dreams, the tendency will be for you to exceed your limitations. Be aware that the potential that exists in you is limitless and largely untapped.

STEP 6

Plan your priorities.

One thing that all successful people have in common is that they have mastered the ability to manage their time. First and foremost, they have organized themselves. Keep in mind that every minute spent in planning will save you two in execution. In other words, you never regain lost time, so make the most of every moment.

STEP 7

Sacrifice to Succeed.

Nothing of value comes without sacrifice. Life is filled with critical moments when you have the opportunity to trade one value for another. Keep your eyes open for such moments.